DON'T HUG A CACTUS

THIS BOOK BELONGS TO

____

contact information
Crystal.Marie.Art+Book@gmail.com
Instagram @CrystalMarieArt

The cacti Trio
inspired by Echinopsis Genus

Mustache Tessellation
inspired by The Mexican giant Cardon

Flowering in the Desert
Inspired by the Saguaro Cactus

Momma and pups
Inspired by the Barrel Cactus

KNOWN AS DRAGON FRUIT
THE PITAYA CACTUS

El Nopal

Inspired by the Prickly Pear Cactus

A cup of prickly tea
Inspired by the Peanut Cactus

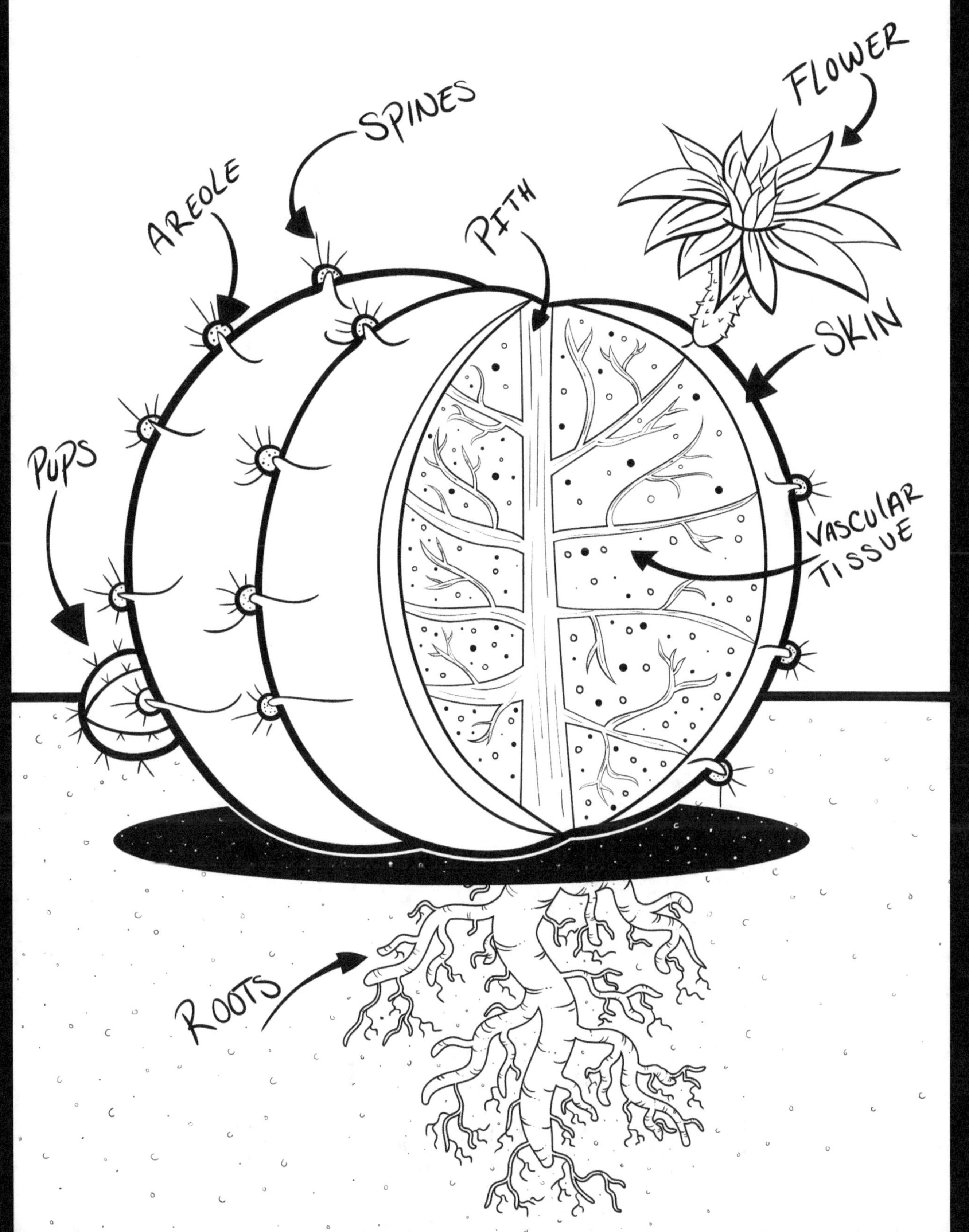

SPINES
AREOLE
PITH
FLOWER
SKIN
PUPS
VASCULAR TISSUE
ROOTS

Cacti Anatomy
Inside the Echinopsis cactus

The collection
Inspired by various Succulents

Señorita Edna

Señor Eduardo

The Starfish
Inspired by the Carrion Cactus

Artfully alive
inspired by Haworthia

Living stones
Inspired by The succulent Lithops

El Churro de Azúcar
Inspired by Cereus Spiralis

Modern Decor
Inspired by The San Pedro Cactus

Las Bolitas
Inspired By tephrocactus geometricus

The Long Good-Bye
Inspired by the Sonoran Desert
Home of the Saguaros